GW01375006

581
Hansen, M.

~ experiment · with ~

THINGS THAT GROW

Mike Halson

Illustrated by Jane Newell
Designed by Steve Page

Consultants: Margaret Rostron, Geoff Puplett and Brian Cook

CONTENTS

ABOUT THIS BOOK	3	GROWING EXPERIMENTS	18 – 29
IMPORTANT THINGS TO REMEMBER	5	Seed needs	18
ALL ABOUT THINGS THAT GROW	6	How seeds grow	20
		Growing without seeds	22
LIGHT EXPERIMENTS	8 – 13	Bottle garden	24
Do plants need light?	8	All about trees	26
How do plants find light?	10	Grow your own vegetables	28
Bubbling plants	12		
WATER EXPERIMENTS	14 – 17	WHAT DO YOU KNOW ABOUT THINGS THAT GROW?	30
Changing colour	14	SCIENCE WORDS	31
Where does all the water go?	16	INDEX	32

British Library Cataloguing in Publication Data
Halson, Michael
Experiment with things that grow.
1. Plants. Physiology. Experiments
I. Title II. Newell, Jane III. Series
581.1'0724
ISBN 0 00 191294 1
ISBN 0 00 190034 X HB

All rights reserved. No part of this publication may be reproduced, stored in a retrieval system, or transmitted, in any form or by any means, electronic, mechanical, photocopying, recording or otherwise, without the prior permission of William Collins Sons & Co Ltd, 8 Grafton Street, LONDON W1X 3LA

William Collins Sons & Co Ltd
London · Glasgow · Sydney · Auckland
Toronto · Johannesburg

First Published in Great Britain 1989
© William Collins Sons & Co Ltd 1989

Printed in Great Britain by Cambus Litho, East Kilbride

ABOUT THIS BOOK

All through history, people have been fascinated by all the amazing things going on around them, and have been trying to find out why and how they happen.

This activity is called science, and the methods used to find things out are called experiments.

Over the centuries, scientists' experiments have helped to answer many questions about our world and the universe.

Because scientists take care to write down exactly what they did, other people can copy their work and find out important facts for themselves.

This book is full of fun-to-do experiments with things that grow. All the activities are simple to do, and only use things which are easy to get hold of.

WHAT YOU WILL NEED

Each experiment tells you all the things you will need. Most of them can be found around the house. Everything else can be bought cheaply from high street stores.

Before you start experimenting, collect together the items you need for the experiments you want to do.

It's a good idea to keep the things you have used for an experiment – many of them will be useful again. You could build up a store of science materials and keep them together in a handy place.

EXPERIMENT TIMES

Some of the experiments have very quick results. But others will take longer – from one day up to two months.

To the left of each experiment is a note telling you how long it will take.

Don't forget that you can do a new experiment while you are waiting for another one to finish.

FINDINGS AND ANSWERS

On page 30, you can find reminders of what you have found out. And on page 31, there are answers to the questions asked on pages 11 and 25.

SCIENCE WORDS

Some of the experiments use words which look like this: *stomata*. These are science words. Find out what they mean and how to say them on page 31.

SCIENCE NOTEBOOK

It's a good idea to keep a special notebook to write down what you have done and found out. This will help you remember what happened. Use drawings as well as words.

4

IMPORTANT THINGS TO REMEMBER

Before you get started, remember that scientists always obey these golden rules:

1 Make sure everything is ready before you start work.

2 Choose a safe area in which to work. It needs to be somewhere where it doesn't matter if you make a mess. A worktop near a sink is a good idea.

3 Always take care about what you are doing. For an experiment to work, each step must be carried out according to the instructions.

4 Wear clothes which can safely be dirtied, with an old shirt or apron on top.

ALL ABOUT THINGS THAT GROW

The experiments in this book are all to do with plants. Plants come in all shapes and sizes, from tiny mosses to huge trees. Many plants can be eaten, but some are poisonous.

This book explains lots of interesting things about the plant world. And as well as making all kinds of scientific discoveries, you will be able to grow your own houseplants, vegetables and even trees!

PLANT PARTS

Like all living things, plants need to eat, breathe and have babies. Each of the parts shown in this picture helps them to do these things.

As you read the book, you will discover more about how plants work. You can check what the experiments show by turning to page 30.

WHAT USE ARE THINGS THAT GROW?

Things that grow play an even larger part in our lives than you might have realized. Think about the objects around you and the things you eat and drink.

How many objects named in the picture are connected with things that grow?

Answer: all of them! They're all products made by humans out of trees, vegetables and other plants! Even this book is made from paper and card, both of which come from trees.

light·experiments

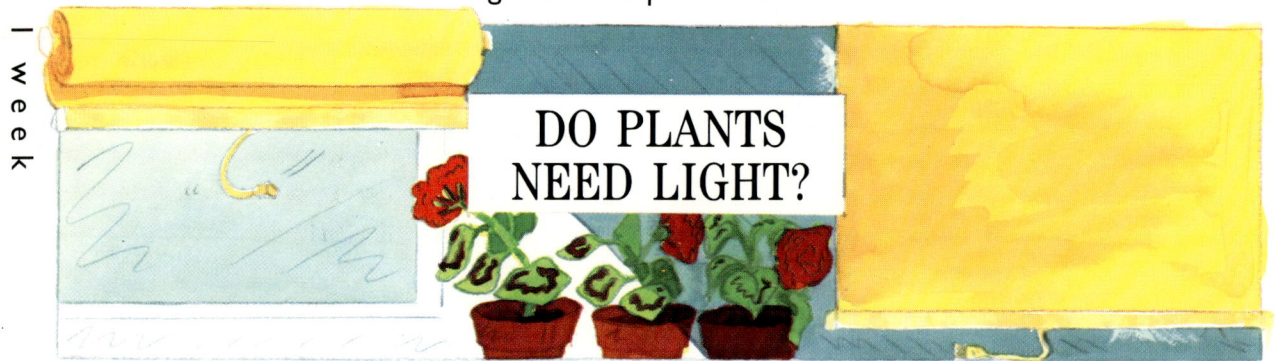

DO PLANTS NEED LIGHT?

1 week

Human beings would be lost without light. They wouldn't be able to see where they were going or what they were doing.

But plants don't move about and they don't have eyes, so do they need light at all?
Here's how to find out.

You will need:
a plant with fairly big leaves
some aluminium foil
scissors

1 Choose a large healthy leaf for your experiment. Cut out a square of foil and fold it in half. Fold over the side edges to make a pocket.

2 Carefully push the pocket over the leaf so only the stalk is showing.

3 Leave the plant in its usual spot for a week, making sure the soil is watered as usual.

8

4 Holding the stalk, pull the pocket away from the leaf. You should be able to see quite a difference!

WHAT HAPPENED AND WHY?
The covered leaf will have become pale and unhealthy looking, while all the others should be the same as before.

Although plants look as though they never really do anything – except grow – they are actually busy all day long.

Unlike animals, plants make their own food. They take all the ingredients they need out of the soil and the air, and turn them into sugar. But to do this, they need one extra thing: light.

The way plants use light to make food is called *photosynthesis*. You can find out more about how it works on pages 10–17.

The substance inside plants which makes them able to trap and use light is called *chlorophyll*. This is green, which is why plants' leaves are mostly green!

The leaf started to die because it could not make any food in the dark. Now that it is back in the light, it should soon start to look its old self again!

INSECT EATERS

In places where it is hard to make food, some plants have found an extra way of feeding themselves. They set a trap for insects in their leaves and then feed on them using special juices.

The plant in the picture, a Venus flytrap, snaps its leaves together like jaws when an insect lands on them.

light·experiments

1 week

HOW DO PLANTS FIND LIGHT?

If you found yourself in a dark place, how would you get back into the light? You would use your eyes to find it and your legs to move towards it.

You will need:
2 containers, marked A and B, filled with bean sprouts*
a cardboard box big enough to cover both containers
some aluminium foil
scissors

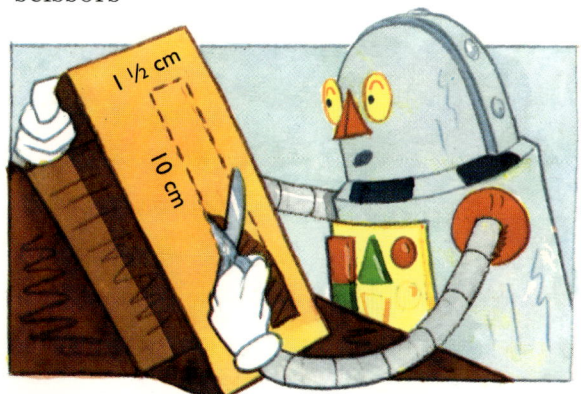

1 Cut a slot 1 ½ cm by 10 cm in the side of the box, as in the picture.

But what about plants? Is there anything they can do to make sure they get enough light to live?

This experiment provides the answer.

2 Now make a foil cover as shown, and place it over all of the bean sprouts in container A.

3 Put the two containers next to each other in a brightly lit place – either natural or electric light will do. A windowsill is a good spot.

10
* See page 29 for how to grow your own bean sprouts. Mustard and cress or oat seedlings are also suitable for this experiment.

4 Place the box over the two containers, with the slot towards the light.

5 After a week, lift up the box and look at the containers. Can you see any differences?

WHAT HAPPENED AND WHY?
The bean sprouts with the cover on will still be growing straight upwards, but the uncovered ones will have bent towards the slot in the side.

This experiment proves that plants <u>can</u> do something to make sure they get more light.

Normally, they grow upwards, towards the sun. But if the light comes from somewhere else, they can quickly change direction.

The uncovered bean sprouts sensed the light coming in from the side and started to grow towards it. If you left them alone for a few more weeks, they would all grow through the slot and into the daylight.

The covered bean sprouts did not start growing towards the light. This shows that the only part that can sense light is right at the top – which was covered by the foil.

OTHER THINGS TO DO
Look at how houseplants on windowsills grow towards the sun. What do you think would happen if you turned the plants round?*

PLANTS IN THE JUNGLE
So many plants grow in the jungle, they compete with each other to get enough light. Many plants grow to a great height to try to catch the sunshine.

* You can find the answer on page 31.

light·experiments

BUBBLING PLANTS

1 hour

During the day, plants spend their time making food for themselves. But they are also doing something else which is very important for humans and all other animals.

This experiment shows you the best way to see what's going on — by using plants which live underwater.

You will need:
a flat bottomed bowl, filled with water (a washing up bowl is ideal)
6 strands of pondweed, taken from a pond or fish tank, or bought from an aquarium shop
a tall, fairly narrow jar

1 Stand the bowl in a brightly lit place, such as next to a window. Put the jar into the water and get rid of all the air, as shown in the picture.

2 Push the weed half way into the jar. Stand the jar on the bottom, as shown, so that the weed is held firmly in place.

3 After 20 minutes, look carefully at the experiment. Does it look any different? If not, wait for another ten minutes and have another look.

WHAT HAPPENED AND WHY?

Tiny bubbles will be coming out of the pondweed. Some will have stuck to the weed or the jar, but others will have risen to the top.

If you have already done the experiment on pages 8 – 9, you will know that when light falls on plants, something called *photosynthesis* starts.

The bubbles coming out of the leaves and stems of the weed are made during photosynthesis. They are a gas called *oxygen*, which is normally invisible and is the most important ingredient of air.

When animals breathe, they take in oxygen and give off another gas called *carbon dioxide*.

During photosynthesis, plants do the opposite. They take in carbon dioxide and give off oxygen.

Without a constant supply of newly made oxygen, there would be no animal life on Earth!

Now that you have done this experiment, can you think why underwater plants are useful in fish tanks?

The answer is that fish, like all other animals, breathe in oxygen, only this time they take it out of water rather than air.

Having plants in a tank is a good way of making sure the fish get all the oxygen they need.

water · experiments

2 hours

CHANGING COLOUR

Water is one of the things which plants need most. Without it, they would soon wilt (go floppy) and then die.

You will need:
6 freshly cut white flowers with stalks (carnations are ideal)
a celery stalk with a few leaves on top
a jar filled with about 2 cm of water
some food colouring or ink
a small spoon

1 Put two spoonfuls of the food colouring or ink into the water. Be very careful – these substances make stains which are hard to remove!
  Stand the stalks in the jar. After only a few minutes you should be able to see something starting to happen.

This experiment shows how water travels round plants. It is also a way of magically changing the colour of cut flowers!

2 After two hours, the flowers will look very different. What has happened to the celery stalk and leaves?

WHAT HAPPENED AND WHY?
The coloured water will gradually have worked its way up the stalks and into the leaves and flowers.

The experiment shows that things that grow suck up water and transport it all through themselves.

14

Normally, this happens through the roots, which take water out of the soil. But as you can see, even when the roots have been cut off, plants can take in water perfectly well.

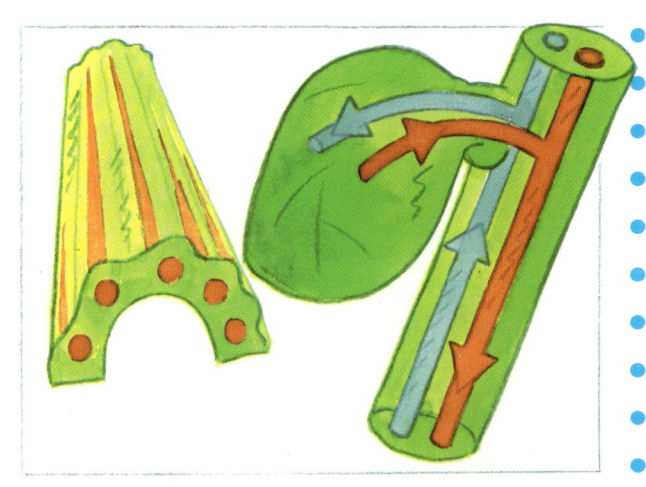

If you snap the celery stalk in half, you will see that plants don't just suck up water like a sponge. Instead, the water passes up special tubes to the leaves and flowers. There are other tubes which carry round the food made in the leaves.*

WHY DO PLANTS NEED WATER?
Plants need water for three main reasons.

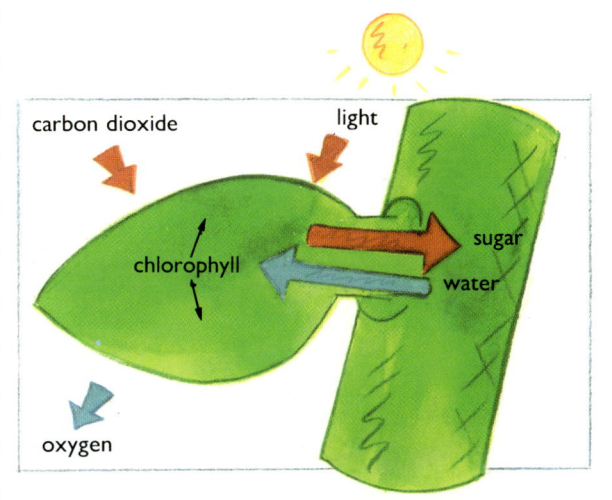

1   As an ingredient in *photosynthesis*.**
The picture above shows how photosynthesis works.

2   Water is the major ingredient in plants. In fact, almost all plants are at least 90% water and only 10% solid matter. Not that humans are much different: we too are about 75% water!

3   As for the third use for water – you'll have to do the experiment on pages 16 – 17 to find that out!

MORE ABOUT ROOTS
Roots are extremely important to plants. Here are two reasons why:
1   They hold the plant firmly in place.
2   By growing in all directions they give the plant a better chance of finding water.

* See pages 8 – 9 for more on food.   ** See also pages 8 – 13.

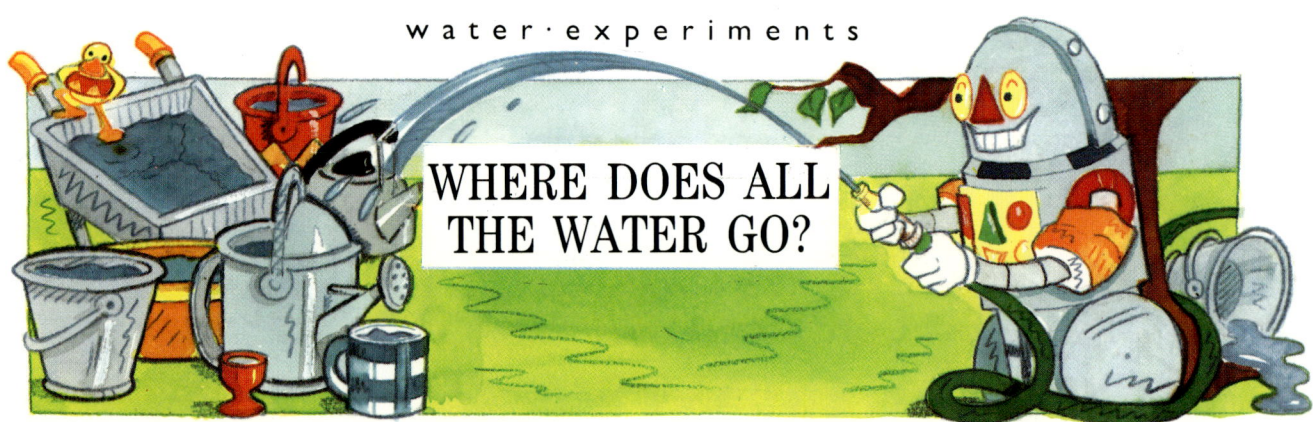

water · experiments

WHERE DOES ALL THE WATER GO?

Things that grow get through a lot of water. An ordinary tree can drink about 50 buckets in just one day! Houseplants too need constant watering to keep them alive.

Why do you think plants need this

You will need:
a houseplant which has been recently watered (don't use a plant which has hairy leaves)
a clear plastic bag large enough to cover the plant
a piece of string or cotton
a magnifying glass

huge amount of water? It's not for making food or growing – that only uses up quite a small amount.

This experiment gives the answer to the puzzle.

1 Cover the plant, but not the pot, with the bag. Using the string or cotton, tie the bag tightly at the base of the stem so it is airtight.

2 Stand the pot in bright light (sunlight if possible) for two hours. Look carefully at the bag. Can you see what has happened?

WHAT HAPPENED AND WHY?
The plastic bag will be covered on the inside with tiny drops of water.

The water came out of holes in the leaves called *stomata*. You will be able to see the stomata through the magnifying glass.

The way a plant loses water is called *transpiration*. This helps in three ways:
1 Water lost from the leaves helps keep the plant cool.
2 The lost water makes room for more water to come up through the plant's roots. In the water are salts which have dissolved out of the soil. These are needed to help the plant grow.
3 A constant supply of water is needed for *photosynthesis** and for forming the plant itself.

Using water to stay cool isn't just something plants do. Humans and other animals do it too. This time, instead of being called transpiration, it's called *sweating*.

DID YOU KNOW?
One of the most familiar sights during autumn is linked to transpiration.

As the weather gets colder, trees and shrubs aren't able to take in much water from the ground. So to avoid losing the water they already contain, many of them close off all the outlets – simply by getting rid of all their leaves!

growing·experiments

SEED NEEDS

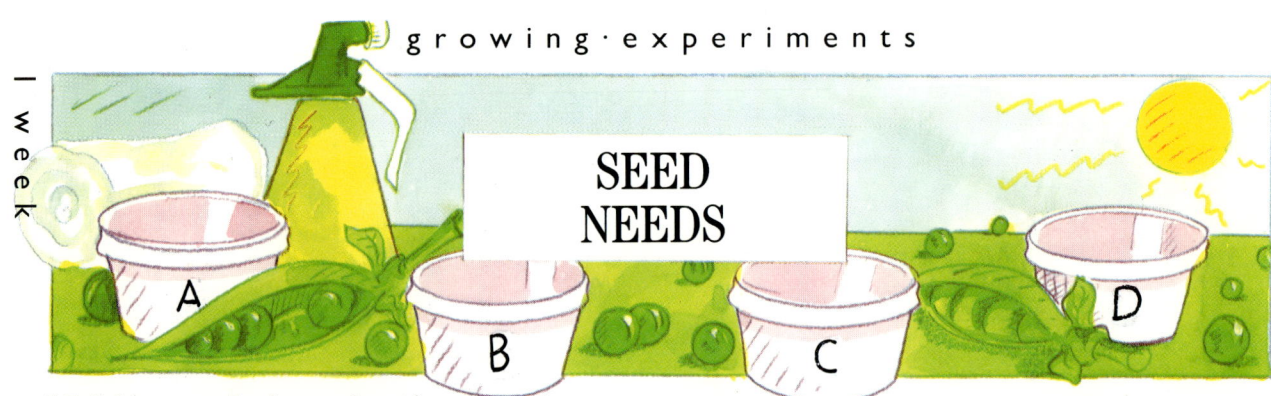

1 week

Making seeds is a plant's way of producing babies. The seeds are produced inside its flowers and form part of the plant's fruit.

pea seeds

Seeds contain a baby plant and a food store, well protected inside a strong skin.

Seeds will not develop, or *germinate*, unless the conditions are right. They may have to wait months or even years.

This experiment shows you what a seed needs to make it grow into a seedling.

You will need:
6 pea seeds (these must be proper packet seeds, not frozen, tinned or fresh peas)
18 pea seeds soaked overnight in a glass of water
4 small containers (margarine tubs are ideal) labelled A, B, C and D
some cotton wool

1 Line each of the containers with a layer of cotton wool. Put the six dry pea seeds into container A.

2 Dampen the cotton wool in containers B, C and D and put six of the soaked seeds into each of them.

18

3 Put container B into a refrigerator. Next, fill container C with water until the seeds are completely covered.

4 Stand containers A, C and D next to each other in a warm place. Leave the four containers alone for a week. Which sets of seeds do you think will germinate?

WHAT HAPPENED AND WHY?

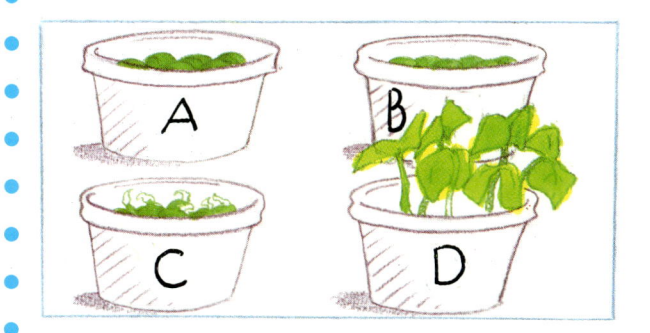

- Only the seeds in container D will have germinated properly.
- Nothing at all will have happened to the seeds in containers A and B.
- The seeds in container C may have started to germinate, but they will not be doing very well.

What were the magic ingredients in container D which were missing in the others?
- The seeds in container A had no <u>water</u>.
- The seeds in container B had no <u>warmth</u>.
- The seeds in container C had no <u>air</u>.
- The seeds in container D had all three!

So you can see from the experiment that to germinate, seeds need three things: water, warmth and air. If just one of these is missing, proper germination will not happen.

GROW YOUR OWN PEA PLANTS

Instead of throwing away the pea seedlings in container D, you can grow them into plants. Find out how on page 28.

growing·experiments

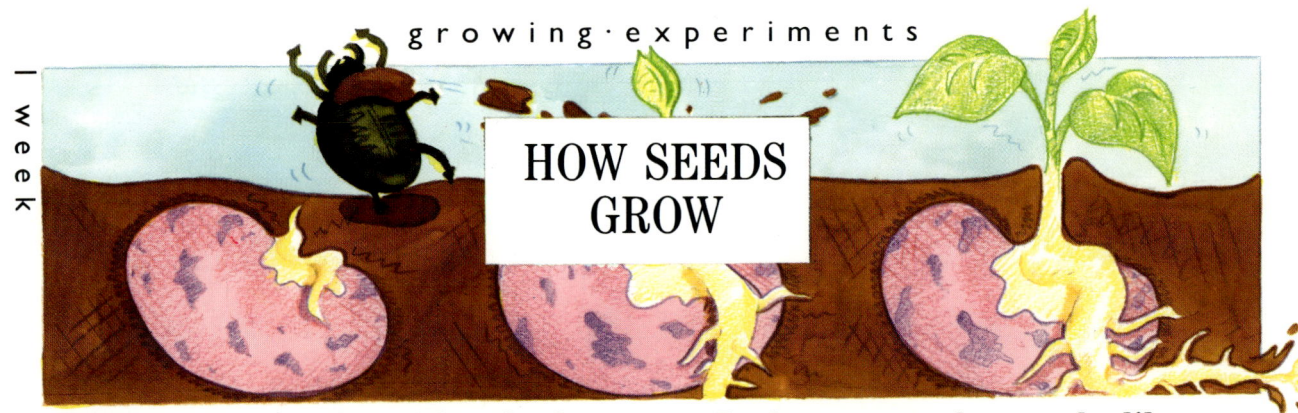

1 week

HOW SEEDS GROW

This experiment takes a close look at what happens when seeds *germinate*.*

It also proves that seeds, like plants, are very good at looking after themselves.

You will need:
a jar
4–6 bean seeds soaked in water overnight (broad beans are ideal)
a strip of blotting paper, 30 cm by 10 cm

1 Dampen the blotting paper, roll it up and put it into the jar so it presses against the sides.

2 Push the beans between the paper and the jar, about half-way down. Put them so they all face in different directions, as shown in the picture.

3 Over the next week, keep looking to see what is happening. Make a note of what appears first, and what appears after that. In which directions do things grow?

* See pages 18–19.

WHAT HAPPENED AND WHY?

The first thing to appear from each seed was a root, searching for water. This was followed by a yellowy green shoot. The root grew downwards and the shoot upwards.

Whichever way a seed is facing, the root and shoot will always grow in these directions. This is because the seed expects water to be in the soil below it and the light to be coming from above.

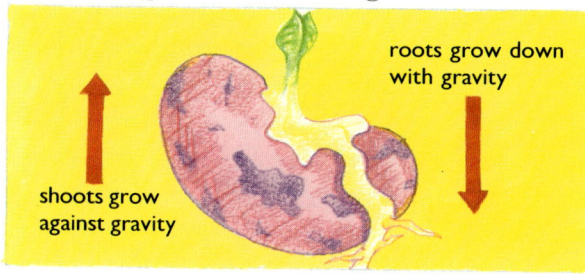

roots grow down with gravity

shoots grow against gravity

The seeds could tell which way was up and which was down because of *gravity*. Gravity is an invisible force which pulls things downwards.

All the seeds had to do was to send their roots in the same direction as gravity and their shoots in the opposite direction.

MORE ABOUT SEEDS

As long as they stay dry, seeds can live for an amazing time.

Seeds over 10,000 years old have been found in Canada. When they were planted, they germinated and grew into Arctic lupins!

DID YOU KNOW?

As well as being sensitive to light and gravity, plants also react to touch and sound.

Scientists have shown that plants grow faster when there is sound, such as music, all around them.

Many people believe that their plants enjoy being talked to and having their leaves touched!

GROW YOUR OWN BEAN PLANTS

Turn to page 28 to find out how to grow your bean seedlings into plants.

growing·experiments

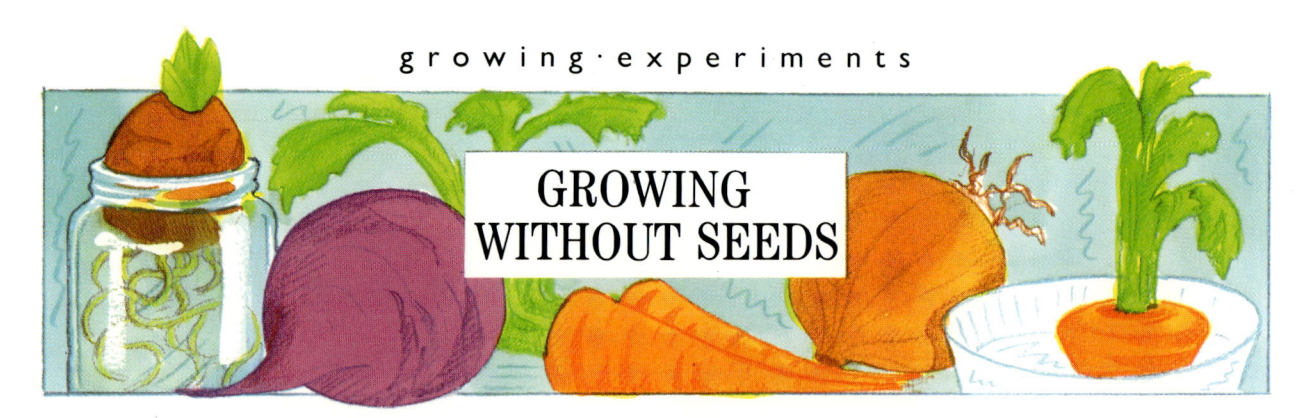

GROWING WITHOUT SEEDS

Growing from seeds is not the only way of producing a new plant.

In this experiment you will find out two other ways for plants to grow. You will also see how things which seem to be dead are really very much alive!

6–8 weeks

GROWING FROM BULBS
You will need:
a hyacinth bulb
a jar small enough for the bulb to sit on top

1 Fill the jar with water, and place the bulb on top. The water should just cover the bottom of the bulb.

2 Put the jar in a cool, dark place and leave it there for four to eight weeks. Have a look from time to time to see the shoots and roots growing, and add extra water if necessary.

3 When the shoots are 2–3 cm high, bring the jar back into the light. Keep it in a cool, light place. The bulb will soon produce large, sweet-smelling flowers.

WHAT ARE BULBS?
To live through the winter, plants must have a way of storing food to keep them going until the weather becomes warmer again.

A good place to store food is underground, where temperatures stay slightly higher than above the surface.

Some plants store food underground by making a bulb. This is the bottom part of the stem, which is surrounded by short, thick leaves.

brown outside leaf

short leaves containing food

During the warm months, the plant sends food to the bulb and makes it swell up. As winter approaches, the part of the plant above the soil shrivels up and dies, leaving only the bulb alive.

In the spring, a new stem and leaves start to grow out of the bulb and form a new plant.

EATING BULBS

Some bulbs are used as food. Two of the best known bulbs which can be eaten are onions and garlic.

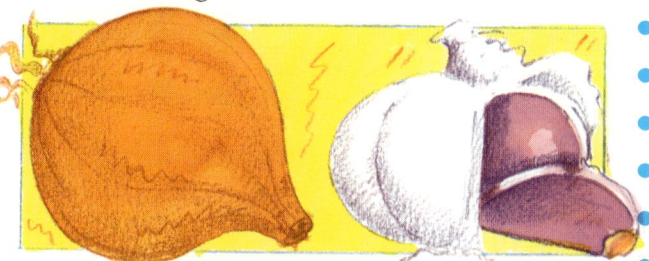

GROWING FROM ROOT VEGETABLE TOPS

1 week

You will need:
3 uncooked root vegetables, such as a carrot, a parsnip and a beetroot
a shallow container filled with a small amount of water

1 Cut off the top 3 cm of each of the vegetables.

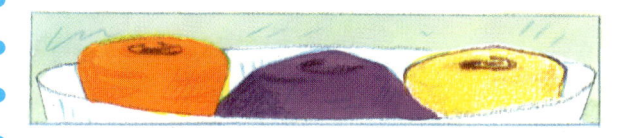

2 Simply place the three vegetable tops in the container as shown.

3 Leave the container in a warm, light place for a week, adding extra water if necessary. The tops should soon produce attractive new leaves.

WHAT ARE ROOT VEGETABLES?

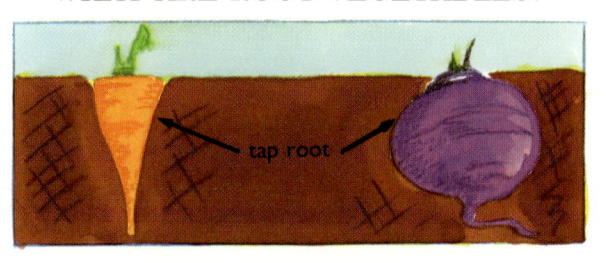

tap root

Root vegetables are another kind of underground food store. Plants such as carrots store food in a large root called a tap root to last them through the winter.

23

growing·experiments

1 hour

BOTTLE GARDEN

How would you like to have your own indoor garden? On these two pages you can find out how to set up an attractive garden inside a plastic or glass container.

You will need:
a large jar,* if possible with a screw-on top (if you cannot find one with a top, use clingfilm instead)
some pebbles
some charcoal pieces 1–2 cm long (you can use barbecue charcoal)
some potting compost
a large serving spoon
a water sprayer
5 different baby plants, no more than 5–6 cm high (good plants to use are ferns, ivies, African violets and begonias)

1 Make sure the jar is clean and dry. Lay it on its side and cover the bottom with a layer of pebbles.

2 On top of the pebbles, add a layer of charcoal pieces.

3 Next, add a layer of potting compost, using the spoon. Make a layer 3 cm deep, with one or two hilly bits. Pat the compost down firmly.

24

* The jar opening must be big enough to get your hand in easily.

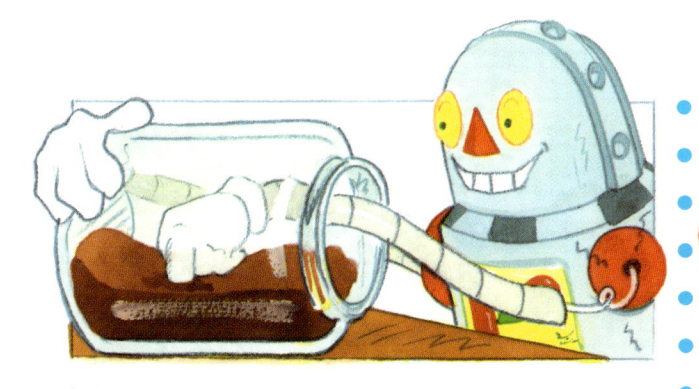

4 Decide where to put the plants and in what order you need to plant them. Make a hole in the compost where the first plant is to go.

5 Hold the first plant upside down and gently remove it from its pot.

6 Press the plant into the hole and fill in any spaces with the compost. Do the same with the other plants.

7 When everything is in place, wipe off any compost which has stuck to the side of the jar. Then, spray two or three squirts of water over the plants. If there is a top, put it in place. Otherwise, stretch a piece of clingfilm over the opening to make it airtight.

8 Next day, if the level of moisture is right, there should be a film of water on the inside of the jar. If not, spray more water inside. If there is so much water it is difficult to see the plants, wipe it off with a tissue.

9 Keep your bottle garden in a warm, light place where there is not much sunlight. It should need hardly any attention – and no watering at all!

TEST YOUR KNOWLEDGE
Can you think why a film of water forms on the inside of the jar? And why don't you need to water your bottle garden?*

* You can find the answer on page 31.

25

growing·experiments

ALL ABOUT TREES

Trees are the largest plants of all. There are thousands of different types, ranging in height from six to over 100 metres!

These experiments will help you find out more about trees and show how to grow your own trees from seeds.

WHAT ARE TREES MADE OF?

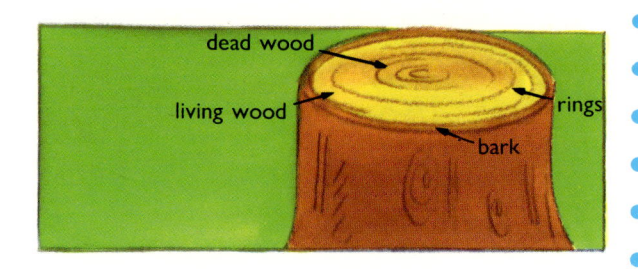

dead wood
living wood
rings
bark

Find a sawn-off tree stump like the one shown. Look at the top of the stump. The picture shows the main things to look out for.

The tree was made of a series of wooden rings. This is because, instead of growing non-stop, the tree grew at different speeds depending on the time of year.

After growing rapidly in the spring, it gradually slowed down until the winter came and it stopped altogether.

Each time it started growing again, an extra ring of wood was added to the outside of the tree.

HOW TO FIND OUT A TREE'S AGE
How old do you think the tree was when it was cut down? There is a simple way to check the answer.

Each year, the tree grew an extra ring. This means that the number of rings is the same as the tree's age. So all you have to do is count the rings!

Was your guess a good one? And how much smaller was the tree when you were born?

HOW TO GROW YOUR OWN TREE

Would you like to plant some trees which will still be around when you have children and grandchildren of your own?

Until they are big enough to be planted outside, the baby trees can be kept inside as houseplants.

You will need:
any of these seeds:
  acorn, horse chestnut, beech nut, hazel nut*, walnut*
  apple or pear pips
  peach*, plum* or cherry* stones
small plant pots filled with moist
  potting compost

1 Soak the seeds in warm water and leave them there for three days.

2 Place one seed in the middle of each pot, about 1 cm from the top.

3 Leave the pots somewhere cool and airy such as a windowsill or balcony (if the weather is warm). Water the soil from time to time to keep it moist.

4 After a few months, the seedlings will start to look like young trees. When they have grown too large for their pots, move them to larger ones.

Once the seedlings are 30 – 60 cm tall, they will be ready to plant outside (ask an adult where they should go). With luck, your trees will still be there in 100 years' time!

It may take a month or two for some of the seeds to *germinate*, so don't be impatient. Some may never germinate at all, which is why it is a good idea to use several different kinds.

* These should all be gently cracked with nut crackers before they are soaked.

27

growing·experiments

GROW YOUR OWN VEGETABLES

a few months

GROWING PEA AND BEAN PLANTS
If you have done the experiments on pages 18–19 and 20–21, you will have a number of seedlings which need looking after.

The packets will tell you the times of year when they can be planted outside. If the weather is cold, you may need to keep them indoors in pots for a while first.

With luck, your bean and pea plants will produce a small crop of peas and beans which you can eat.

You will need:
a few pea and bean seedlings
some canes about 60 cm long
string and scissors
a spoon
a suitable area of soil outside,
  either in a garden or a window box

1 First plant the pea seedlings. In your chosen spot, use the spoon to scoop out a hole. Put in one seedling and replace the soil around it.

2 Plant the other seedlings in the same way, putting them about 10–15 cm apart. Pour water around the seedlings, being careful not to disturb them.

3 Push a cane into the ground next to each seedling. Then, join the canes together as shown, to give the peas something to grow along.

28

4 Plant the beans in the same way as the peas. This time, the canes do not need to be joined together. As the bean plants grow, tie them to the canes for support.

GROWING BEAN SPROUTS

2 weeks

Bean sprouts are some of the fastest things you can grow. You can eat them in salads or sandwiches after less than two weeks!

You will need:
a plastic container, lined with damp cotton wool
any of these bean seeds: mung beans; aduki beans; chick peas; alfalfa; whole lentils; fenugreek seeds
a cup filled with cold water
a sieve
a plastic bag
some newspaper

1 Pour a few dozen seeds into the cup and leave them to soak overnight.

2 Next morning, empty the seeds into the sieve and rinse them under the cold tap.

3 Spread the seeds evenly over the cotton wool. Then, put the container into the plastic bag, and wrap the whole thing up in the newspaper.

4 The beans will soon sprout and will be ready to eat in about a week's time – when they are 30 – 35 mm long. To pick them, simply cut the bean sprouts off near the bottom with scissors.

29

WHAT DO YOU KNOW ABOUT THINGS THAT GROW?

Look again at the picture on page 6. All it told you was the names of the main parts of a plant.

If you have done all the experiments on pages 8 – 27, you will know what each part is for.

Here is the same picture again, but now with some extra information.

All of these facts can be found somewhere in this book.

Leaves:
Leaves are where plants make their food, by *photosynthesis*. They also give off water through *transpiration*.

Stem:
The stem holds up the rest of the plant and lifts it towards the light. It contains tubes which carry water or food round the plant. In trees, the stem is woody and forms the trunk and branches.

Fruit:
Fruits grow around seeds to protect them. Some fruits can be eaten; others cannot.

- Flower:
Flowers are the parts of a plant which produce the seeds.

- Roots:
Roots grow into the soil to take in the water and salts which the plant needs to grow and make food. They also hold the plant firmly to the ground.

SCIENCE WORDS

Carbon dioxide
Say: car-bon die-ox-ide
Carbon dioxide is a gas found in the air. It is used up by plants in photosynthesis.

Chlorophyll
Say: klora-fill
A green substance in plants which allows them to use light to make food.

Germinate
Say: germ-in-ate
Seeds germinate when they start to grow into young plants.

Gravity
Gravity is the force which pulls objects towards the Earth. If you throw something into the air, it is gravity which makes it fall back to the ground.

Oxygen
Say: oxy-jen
A gas found in water and air, used for breathing. It is produced by plants during photosynthesis.

Photosynthesis
Say: foe-toe-sinth-iss-iss
Photosynthesis is the way plants make their food, using light from the sun.

Stomata
Say: sto-marta
Stomata are the tiny holes in leaves used in transpiration.

Sweating
Humans and other animals sweat when they are hot to help them cool down. Sweat is mostly water and leaves the body through tiny holes in the skin.

Transpiration
Say: tran-spirr-ay-shun
Transpiration is the way plants pass water into the air through their leaves.

ANSWERS TO THE QUESTIONS ON PAGES 11 AND 25

Page 11
If you turned the plants round, they would change direction and start to grow back towards the light.

Page 25
A film of water forms because of *transpiration* (see pages 16–17). You don't need to water the bottle garden because the water lost in transpiration runs back into the soil.
   Only a tiny amount of water is actually used up by the plants.

Index

air 9, 12, 13, 19, 31
animals 12, 13, 17, 31
Arctic lupins 21
autumn 17

babies 6, 18
bean plants 21, 28
bean seeds 20-21
bean sprouts 10-11, 29
beetroot 23
bottle garden 24-25, 31
branches 30
breathing 6, 13, 31
bubbles 12-13
bulbs 22-23

Canada 21
carbon dioxide 13, 15, 31
carnations 14
carrot 23
celery 14-15
chlorophyll 9, 15, 31
clothes for experiments 5
colour 14
cut flowers 14

experiment times 4
experiments 3, 4, 5

fish 13
fish tank 12, 13
flowers 6, 14-15, 18, 22
food 9, 12, 15, 18, 22, 23, 30, 31
food colouring 14
fruit 6, 18, 30

garlic 23
gas 13, 31
germination 18-19, 20-21, 27, 31
gravity 21, 31

houseplants 6, 11, 16, 27
humans 7, 12, 15, 17, 31
hyacinth 22

ink 14
insect eaters 9
insects 9
items for experiments 3

jungle 11

leaves 6, 8-9, 13, 14-15, 16-17, 23, 30, 31
light 8-9, 10-11, 12-13, 15, 16, 21, 22, 30, 31

magnifying glass 16-17
mosses 6
music 21

onions 23
oxygen 13, 15, 31

paper 7

parsnip 23
pea plants 19, 28
pea seeds 18-19
photosynthesis 9, 13, 15, 17, 30, 31
plant parts 6, 30
plant products 7
plant world 6
pondweed 12-13

refrigerator 19
root vegetables 23
roots 6, 15, 17, 21, 22-23, 30

salts 17, 30
salads 29
sandwiches 29
science 3
science materials 3
science notebook 4
science rules 5
science words 4, 31
scientist 3, 5, 21
seedlings 10, 18, 19, 21, 27, 28
seeds 18-19, 20-21, 22, 26, 27, 29, 30, 31
shoot 21, 22
shrubs 17
soil 9, 15, 17, 21, 23, 30, 31
sound 21
spring 23, 26
stalks 14
stem 6, 13, 16, 23, 24, 30

stomata 4, 16, 31
sugar 9, 15
sun 11, 31
sweating 17, 31

tap root 23
things that grow 3, 6-7, 16, 30
touch 21
transpiration 16, 30, 31
tree age 26
tree rings 26
tree stump 26
trees 6, 7, 16, 17, 26-27, 30
trunk 30
tubes 15, 30

underwater plants 12-13

vegetables 6, 7, 23, 28-29
Venus flytrap 9

warmth 19
water
  in plants 14-15, 16-17, 30, 31
  in humans and other animals 15, 31
  in seeds 19
  in soil 21, 30
wilt 14
winter 23, 26